Free catalogue!

Dolls to treasure, books to read and read again, clothes for every occasion... the American Girl® catalogue is full of all the things girls love! To join our mailing list, call 1-800-845-0005, or visit our Web site at americangirl.com.

12583i

▲ Detach here before mailing ▲

Try it risk-free!

American Girl® magazine is especially for girls 8 and up. Send for your preview issue today! Mail this card to receive a risk-free preview issue and start your one-year subscription. For just $19.95, you'll receive 6 bimonthly issues in all! If you don't love it right away, just write "cancel" on the invoice and return it to us. The preview issue is yours to keep, free!

Send bill to: (please print)

_____
adult's name

_____
address

_____
city   state   zip

_____
adult's signature

Send magazine to: (please print)

_____   /   /   ____
girl's name   birth date

_____
address

_____
city   state   zip

Guarantee: You may cancel at any time for a full refund. Allow 4–6 weeks for first issue. Non-U.S. subscriptions $24 U.S., prepaid only.
© 2001 Pleasant Company

K14L7

Join our mailing list to receive the American Girl
catalogue. It's full of all the things girls love!

To get your free catalogue, call 1-800-845-0005
or visit our Web site at americangirl.com.

Pleasant Company, 8400 Fairway Place, Middleton, WI 53562

12583i

Letter to You

You can **make just about anything** with
salt dough. Create something big or small, flat or round.
It's **simple to do,** and, most likely, you already have
everything you need in your kitchen right now:
flour, water, and salt!
Whip up a batch, then follow the easy instructions.
Having fun is as **easy as 1-2-3!**

Contents

The Recipe

Set out 2 cups of **all-purpose flour,** 1 cup of **salt,** 1 cup of warm **water**—and a **bowl.**

1. Stir the **water** and **salt** together. Let stand for about 1 minute to let the salt dissolve.

2. Add the **flour** and **stir**. When the dough becomes too stiff to stir, use your hands.

3. Spill the dough onto a hard floured surface and **knead** it. (To knead dough, hold it with one hand while you push it away from you with the other. Then fold it back on itself.)

4. The dough should feel soft, not sticky. You may have to add more flour. Keep kneading until the dough is smooth. **Store** it in a plastic bag so it stays soft as you are working.

The Secret

For best results, use **foil in the middle** to reduce cooking time and to give your project a sturdy shape.

1. If a project is thicker than 1 inch, ball up **foil** or form it into the desired shape.

2. Dust a **rolling pin** or your hands with flour, and flatten a piece of dough until it's about ¼-inch thick.

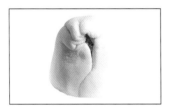

3. Wrap the dough around the foil, gently pressing it into shape. Remove extra dough with a **butter knife.**

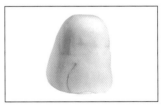

4. To make seams disappear, dip your finger in **water** and smooth them out.

THE RIGHT TOUCH

These **tips and tricks** will help guarantee your project looks its best **right out of the oven!**

Work directly on a cookie sheet so you won't have to move the project to get it in the oven.

Make sure your project has a sturdy base so it won't tip over in the oven.

Use a little water to attach ears, arms, and other parts. Water will make the dough stick together better.

Before baking dough with any decoration, such as wire, paper, or beads, check with an adult. If it's O.K., bake the project at 200 degrees. You can also use craft glue to attach the decorations to your dough project after it has baked.

If your project needs a little help staying in the right position, use wads of foil to prop it up in the oven.

BAKING

Bake salt dough projects on a **cookie sheet** at **200 degrees** for 1 to 4 hours.

Projects should stay in the oven until they are dry and hard. Larger projects will take longer than smaller projects.

With an adult's help, remove the cookie sheet with **oven mitts.** Move the baked dough to a cooling rack.

REPAIRS

If a project cracks or a piece falls off, you can always **repair the damage** before you paint it.

Fill in a crack or reattach a part with unbaked dough. Smooth unbaked salt dough into place with water.

Keep adding and smoothing dough until the whole crack is covered. Re-bake until the new dough is hard and dry.

Finishing

After the project cools, you must **seal it,** or the dough will crack from moisture in the air.

Projects will last longer if you seal them. Acrylic paint works for a short time. For best results, after the paint dries, use an acrylic spray or a sealant, like Mod Podge, available from a craft store. You can also make your own sealant by mixing 1 tablespoon of Elmer's glue with 1 tablespoon of water. Paint the project completely with the mixture and let dry.

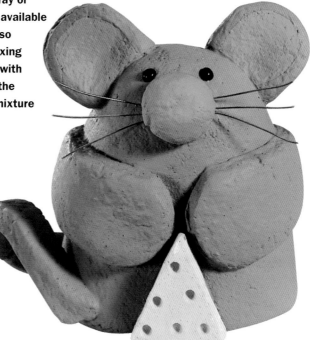

GREAT MISTAKES!

Did your project sag, droop, wrinkle, or bend over backward? **Don't worry about it!**

If you follow the directions carefully, your projects should come out just as you put them in the oven, only slightly puffier. It helps to keep projects simple. Later you can add details with paint. But sometimes salt dough does funny things. A project might shrink or tilt. This gives each project its own personality. No two will ever be exactly alike! And that is what makes salt dough so special.

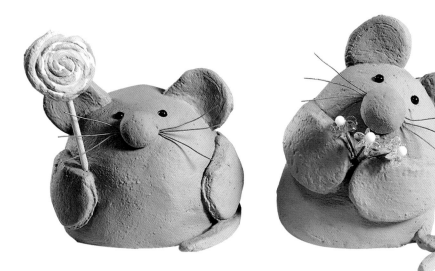

GO WILD!

Create the **kookiest creatures** from land or sea, and soon you'll have **a menagerie!**

Frog Cover a foil ball with rolled-out dough. Attach a smaller ball for a head. Add balls for eyes. Carve a mouth with a butter knife. Stick in a plastic-coated wire for a tongue. Use long hearts for feet, dividing toes with a butter knife.

Pig Cover a foil ball with rolled-out dough. Add a teardrop-shaped head, flattening the pointed end with your finger for a snout. Finish with bead eyes, triangle ears, oval legs, and a beaded flower, if desired.

Octopus Shape foil like a pear and cover it with rolled-out dough. Add oval eyes with bead pupils. Stick on triangle-shaped lips. Attach rope legs. Curl up one leg and make suckers with the flat end of a skewer.

Fish Cover a flat foil oval with rolled-out dough. Add heart, oval, or triangle fins. Flatten balls for eyes. Press in the center of an oval with a butter knife for lips.

Elephant Cover a foil oval with rolled-out dough. Add a teardrop-shaped head, lengthening the point. Attach pancake ears, ball feet, and a wire tail. Use a wad of foil to hold up the trunk while it's baking.

Clam Flatten dough into a large oval. Fold it over a foil ball in a clam shape. Attach ball eyes. Add a dough ball for a pearl.

PLANT PALS

Perk up **potted plants** or flowers with garden-variety **creepy crawlies.**

Butterfly Make a tube shape. Attach teardrop, oval, or circle wings. Use wire for antennae.

Snail Make a rope and curl it. Shape one end into a head. Add antennae.

Caterpillar Press balls together for a body. Add antennae.

Ladybug Flatten 2 balls for the head and body. Cut a circle from rolled-out dough, and cut it in half. Place each half on the body for wings. Flatten balls for dots.

Bee Shape a fat oval. Add ball eyes and oval wings.

Note: Before baking, stick a wire into the bottom of each bug for support. Be careful not to get bugs wet when watering plants.

17

The Bunny Bunch

Roll dozens of dough balls into a **bunny family** that can keep growing and growing and growing . . .

Shape 3 balls for the head, body, and cottontail. Press them together. Attach oval legs and ears. Use tiny balls for the cheeks and nose.

Fiesta Flowers

For a **touch of color** in your room, display a pot of daisies, tulips, and other **beautiful blooms.**

Vase Shape a vase from foil, pressing the bottom flat. Cover with rolled-out dough, but leave the top uncovered. Work extra dough up to the top of the vase and shape a mouth opening. After baking and painting, arrange flowers inside.

Flowers Use teardrops or flattened balls for petals. Flatten small balls for flower centers. Before baking, stick a piece of wire into the bottom of each flower for a stem.

FRAME OF MIND

When a **favorite face** deserves more than a plain frame, show it off in a **one-of-a-kind** creation.

Cut a shape from rolled-out dough. Cut another shape inside to fit your photo. Press a frame hook onto the back, if desired. Decorate the frame with extra dough. After baking, paint, then tape your photo to the back of the frame.

MIRROR IMAGE

Shape and bake a **reflection of your style**
on a hand or purse mirror.

Press a small mirror into rolled-out dough. Push the dough against the mirror's edges to overlap slightly, then cut a design around the mirror. Insert a frame hook onto the back, if desired. Add dough decorations.

Desert Dancers

Start this project **from the ground up,** shaping
snakes and lizards that are on the run.

Snake Make a long rope. Curl it into
any snaky shape.

Lizard Start with a fat rope, then
shape a lizard head and tail. Flatten and
shape small ropes into legs and feet.
Decorate with extra dough.

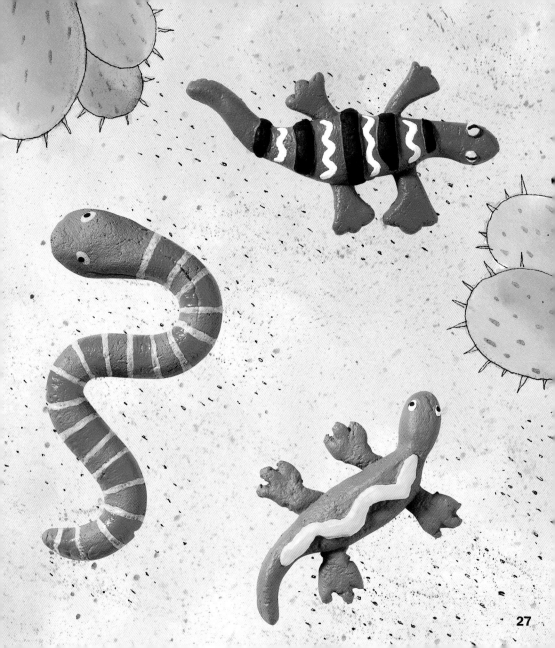

HOME TWEET HOME

Bring the outdoors in with a **birdhouse.** This colorful craft will brighten any **windowsill!**

Shape a house from foil, and cover it with rolled-out dough. You may need several pieces to cover a large house or a house with a large roof. Press the flat part of a bottle cap into the dough to make "bird holes." Insert skewer pieces for perches. Add dough decorations.

Mouse Trap!

Send **mini mice** scurrying for safety before these **fat cats** pounce on them!

Mouse Make an oval. Add flattened balls for ears. Curl a piece of plastic-coated wire into a tail, and press it into the dough.

Cat Press 2 balls side-by-side for the body and head. Make oval legs. Add a fat rope for the tail. Use balls for the cheeks and nose, and add triangles for the ears.

Shelf-Expression

These silly **leg-swinging** critters love life on the edge.

Wrap a foil birdy shape with rolled-out dough. Attach a beak or other accent. Shape the feet, then use a skewer to make a hole that's bigger than your string's thickness. After baking and cooling, thread the feet onto strings, tying the knots in back. Cut the strings so they're equal lengths. Use craft glue to stick the strings to the bottom of your bird, making sure the feet swing forward.

Counting Sheep

Spin some wool for these **sweet sheep,** and when it's **time to sleep,** start counting . . .

Wrap a foil ball with rolled-out dough, but leave the bottom uncovered. Attach an oval head. Cut a long, thin rope into sections. Curl the sections into curlicues, and press them on the sheep, covering the body. Add ears, bangs, or a bow. After baking, press skewer pieces into the bottom foil for legs, if desired. If a leg wobbles, squeeze craft glue into the leg hole, and then insert the skewer.

Happy Birthday!

It's a **birthday party,** so bake a **cake—**
and **presents,** and **hats,** and more!

Cake Shape a foil cake, pressing in a triangle (so it looks like a slice is missing), and cover it with rolled-out dough. Make a plate from flattened dough. Place the cake on top. Stick a toothpick into the cake's center for a candle hole. Decorate with dough.

Hat Fold paper into a cone, then cover the outside with rolled-out dough. Remove the paper after baking. Glue curling ribbon to the top.

Gift bag Shape a rectangular bag. Use wire for handles and curling ribbon for party favors.

Noisemaker Roll up a thin strip of dough. Shape a small cone and attach it to the end of the roll.

Cake slice Shape a dough wedge the size of your cake. Make a plate from flattened dough. Decorate.

Piping Hot

Fresh from the oven, tiny **pretzels, pastries,** and **breads** that look good enough to eat!

Pretzels Twist thin ropes of dough into pretzel shapes.

Cinnamon rolls Roll out a square. Sprinkle cinnamon on top. Roll into a tube, cinnamon side in. Slice into rolls. After baking and cooling, squeeze on white fabric paint.

Cookies Cut cookies from rolled-out dough. Wet the tops, and sprinkle on microbeads.

Croissants Roll out a rectangle. Cut it into 2 long triangles. Start at the wide end of each triangle and roll up. Bend into crescent shapes.

FAST FOOD

Grab a quick bite to eat—**hot dogs and hamburgers** with the works!

Ketchup, mustard Add a cone to a cylinder, then blend shapes into a bottle.

Hamburger Shape round buns. Cut a cheese square and a lettuce circle from rolled-out dough. Flatten a ball for a patty. Put it together just the way you like it!

Hot dog Shape a long oval bun, then cut along the center with a butter knife. Open the bun slightly with your fingers. Roll a wiener, and place it in the bun. Bake, let cool, then paint. Use fabric paint for mustard.

SET UP SHOP

Window shoppers will fall in love with these stylish **hat and handbag sets.**

Hats Add pancakes or ropes to hat shapes to form brims. After baking, paint, then decorate with microbeads, feathers, or rhinestones.

Bags Cut pockets or flaps out of rolled-out dough and attach them to purse shapes. Use wire for straps. Decorate to match hats.

ROOM to GROW

Fill a room with **furniture** and finishings that make you **feel at home!**

Sofa and chair Wrap rolled-out dough around a foil rectangle for a sofa and a foil square for a chair. Cut slits for cushions with a butter knife. Add arched backs. For each arm, cut a rectangle from rolled-out dough, roll the end halfway, and attach.

TV and table Cover a foil rectangle with rolled-out dough. Glue beads to straight pins for rabbit ears. For the table, make a larger rectangle, and use balls for the legs.

Fine Dining

This kitchenette's overstuffed fridge and **table for two** will make any **small meal** look appealing.

Table Cut a square from rolled-out dough. Press a ball into each corner. Bend wire legs and stick them into the corner balls. Bake with the tabletop down on the cookie sheet.

Chair Cut a circle from rolled-out dough. Press a heart-shaped chair back onto the circle. Stick wire legs in the bottom. Bake with the chair backs on the cookie sheet. Prop the legs up with foil, if needed.

Refrigerator Cover a foil rectangle with rolled-out dough. Make an indent for the freezer section with the end of a butter knife.

Snuggle Up

Making **a bed** was never this much fun, so why not make **a table, a lamp,** and **bunny slippers,** too!

Bed Shape a rectangle with a rounded top from foil and cover with rolled-out dough. Shape a headboard from flattened dough and press it to the back. For bedposts, roll 2 ropes. Curl one end of each rope, then place them on either side of the headboard. Cut a coverlet from rolled-out dough. Lay it on the bed. Bake a small pillow separately.

Lamp Top a disk with a ball and a rounded rectangle.

Bedside table Cut a large circle from rolled-out dough, drape it over a foil ball, and pleat the edges.

Bunny slippers Shape a fat oval. Make a hole at the end with a pencil eraser. Add oval ears and a tiny ball nose. Make a pair!

HOLD EVERYTHING

Add **color and style** to cans or cardboard **containers** with salt dough.

Box Wrap rolled-out dough around a small cardboard box. Add an extra strip to the top edge to cover it. To make a lid, put the box onto another piece of rolled-out dough, and mark around it with a butter knife. Cut around the mark. Decorate with dough ribbons and a knob.

Pencil holder Wrap rolled-out dough around a tin can or snack-size chips can. Trim the top with a dough strip. Decorate with flattened balls.

Tea Time!

Paint pretty patterns on **cup and saucer sets,**
then display your collection of "fine china."

Teacup With an adult's permission, press rolled-out dough into an old cup. Shape a handle, press it against the cup, but bake it separately. After cooling, remove the dough cup from the real cup, and attach the handle with craft glue.

Saucer Press rolled-out dough onto an old saucer. Push the real cup onto the saucer's center to make a ring. Remove the cup before baking.

Note: For decoration only. Do not drink or eat from tea sets.

Scared Silly!

Stir up screams with a **spooky scene** complete with a **haunted house,** pumpkins, and ghosts. Boo!

Pumpkin Make a dough pumpkin. Add a stem and a snaky vine. Use a butter knife to make creases.

Ghost Cover a foil ball with rolled-out dough. Trim the bottom and shape it into folds. Cut out a tombstone from flattened dough, if desired.

House Make a foil house and cover it with rolled-out dough. Cut the door and other trim from rolled-out dough. Attach a chimney and a peeking ghost.

55

Eye Candy

This **pile of candy** is sweet to look at . . .
and **a treat** to make!

Licorice Twist 2 ropes together. Trim the ends.

Lollipops Roll long ropes, curl each one into a circle and add a skewer.

M&M's, caramels, jelly beans, Kisses Shape candy with fingers. Wrap each Kiss with a paper strip in foil.

Tootsie Rolls, Smarties, mints, jawbreakers Cut triangles from rolled-out dough and shape. Attach to opposite ends of flattened balls or tubes for wrappers.

Sweethearts, Starbursts, Peppermint Patties Roll out a thick layer of dough. Cut out shapes.

"Fa la la la la..."

Angel Cut an angel from rolled-out dough. Add ball cheeks. Flatten a dough rope for the halo or use wire. After baking, loop a wire through the halo to hang.

Snowman Press 2 balls together. Cut a scarf from rolled-out dough. For a hat, press a ball onto a pancake. Attach a cone nose. Before baking, insert a paper clip into the dough to hang.

Turn a tree or garland into a **work of art** with eye-catching **ornaments.**

Teddy bear Attach a small cone to the front of a ball for a head. Use a ball for the nose and flattened balls for ears. Stick the head to a ball body. Make oval arms and thick oval legs. For a bow, put 2 triangle points together, then press a tiny ball in the center. Before baking, insert a paper clip to hang.

Candy cane Roll a rope, and bend it into a candy cane. Before baking, insert a paper clip to hang.

"...la la la la!"

Star Decorate star cutouts with beads, rhinestones, or glitter. Before baking, thread wire through a hole at the top to hang.

Stocking mouse Cut a sock shape from rolled-out dough. Make a ball head, flattened-ball ears, and a ball nose. Press oval arms over the sock. Before baking, insert a paper clip to hang.

Elf hat Shape a cone and bend the top slightly. Add a ball to the tip. Trim the bottom with a flattened dough rope. Before baking, thread wire through a hole at the top to hang.

Sock Cut a sock shape from rolled-out dough. Place dough presents at the top. Trim the sock top with a dough rope. Before baking, thread wire through a hole at the top to hang.

 # Let It Snow!

Keep winter **frozen in time** with a frosty little doughman and *very* curious **penguin pals!**

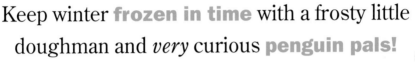

Penguin Shape 2 balls for the head and body. Attach a cone beak, flattened ovals for wings, and oval feet.

Snowman Cover foil balls with rolled-out dough. Stick in skewer arms. Make mittens and add to skewer ends. For a hat, put an oval on top of a pancake, and add a dough ribbon. Press on real buttons and a dough heart.

Let's Share!

Did you make a dough project that you think is unique? Send us a photo! Your idea might show up in one of our publications, so add your name, address, and phone number.

Send photos to:
Salt Dough Editor
American Girl
8400 Fairway Place
Middleton, WI 53562

Published by Pleasant Company Publications

Copyright © 2001 by Pleasant Company

Visit our Web site: **www.americangirl.com**

Printed in Hong Kong.

01 02 03 04 05 06 07 C&C 10 9 8 7 6 5 4 3 2 1

American Girl Library® is a registered trademark of Pleasant Company.

Editorial Development: Trula Magruder, Michelle Watkins
Art Direction: Chris Lorette David
Design: Camela Decaire
Production: Kendra Pulvermacher, Janette Sowinski
Illustrations: Wendy Wallin Malinow
Photography: Jamie Young
Stylists: Camela Decaire, Sarajane Lien

Library of Congress Cataloging-in-Publication Data
Torres, Laura.
Salt dough : just 3 ingredients, more than 100 projects /
[by Laura Torres ; illustrations, Wendy Wallin Malinow].
p. cm. "American girl library."
ISBN 1-58485-370-0
1. Bread dough craft—Juvenile literature. [1. Bread dough craft. 2. Handicraft]
I. Malinow, Wendy Wallin, ill. II. American girl (Middleton, Wis.) III. Title.
TT880 .T66 2001   745.5—dc21   2001022198

Salt Dough

By Laura Torres
Illustrated by Wendy Wallin Malinow